TIME MANAGEMENT

12 SIMPLE TIME MANAGEMENT STEPS TO BETTER FOCUS, FASTER PROGRESS AND OPTIMAL RESULTS. (Personal Health & Wellbeing Book 2)

Disclaimer

This book is only intended as an informational guideline to become more productive and more focused, and should not be considered expert instruction. In serious cases, seek help from a professional healthcare practitioner. All attempts have been made to verify the information listed in this book; however, the author cannot assume any responsibility for any loss, damage or misappropriation of any information herein contained.

Introduction

"Productivity is not just about doing more, it is about creating more impact with less work."
– Prima Malik

Time is a finite commodity; we have only the allotted number of hours in a day to get things done. And if you're anything like the millions of people out there trying to keep up in this always-on, always-connected digital age, it might seem like those hours just aren't enough.

But what if you changed the way you used those hours? The simple fact is that successful people manage their time better. It's not about trying to do more, it's about streamlining what you're already doing – focusing *enough time* on the *right tasks* – and in that way opening up more time for other pursuits, like those things you've always wanted to do, but can never get around to.

That's the topic this book explores: harnessing good time management, sharper focus and correct planning to make every 24 hours as productive as they can possibly be. It's really that easy. You just need to change your approach.

So if you're ready to super-charge what you're really capable of accomplishing every day, let's get started!

Contents

Chapter 1
Why can't I focus?

In the last 20 years or so, the world has made massive strides forward in technology. It's something that touches every aspect of our daily lives – from how we communicate to how we spend our time. And it's something that's moving us into a new and exciting future with uncharted waters. What was considered the norm as little as five years ago has changed, and it will keep changing; many now predict that current and future generations will one day be working in jobs that haven't even been invented yet; our children will study degrees that don't yet exist.

This information-driven and fast-changing society has created the necessity for a new kind of human – one who can handle multiple tasks seemingly at once in a world that never switches off, where multitudes of things demand our attention all at once in a constant sensory barrage of information.

In these frantic times, we'd all like to think we've mastered the ability to multitask – we can talk on the phone, check emails and browse the web all at the same time. But can we really? Unfortunately, the answer is no. It is not physiologically possible for your brain to focus on more than one thing at a time. In fact, the more you shift your focus, the more time you waste by making your brain have to continually readjust itself to something different. But there is a way to stay ahead of the curve: learning how to focus more effectively and manage your time more efficiently.

Let's start at the beginning: in order to really understand how your mind works, and ultimately how you work, you need to have a deeper understanding of the concepts of 'focus', 'attention' and 'distraction'.

Focus and attention

Let's start with the concepts of 'focus' and 'attention':

FOCUS *An act of concentrating interest or activity on something*
ATTENTION *Notice taken of someone or something*

So what do you notice when you look at these definitions? The first thing is that 'focus' requires some kind of action; you have to actively pay attention in an activity to really call it focus. It is intentional. It's when you sit down to type up something on your computer, when you read a book, or when you study for an exam. You can channel your focus towards whatever activity you would like to accomplish.

The amount of time someone can focus on something differs from person to person. Unfortunately, it's not very long. The average attention span is only about five to 20 minutes. Some researchers even theorise that our attention spans have gotten shorter purely because of the hectic lives we now lead; our brains have adapted to have shorter attention spans because we have to focus on so many things throughout the day.

Added to this, because of the high stimulation we get from things like watching TV and browsing the web, we are more easily bored. This can play a huge role when it comes to completing tasks that we find mundane or uninteresting.

But the good news is that you still have control over what you do: when you lose focus, you can simply re-focus on your task again.

On the other hand, in contrast to focus, there is 'attention'; something that you don't necessarily have control over. If someone calls your name, they will automatically have your attention. It is unintentional, and it only lasts a few seconds. It's basically when our brains respond to external stimuli, like movement, light, noise or even pain. Your focus temporarily moves from whatever you were doing to the new intrusion into your world – which comes in handy for keeping you alive, but can hinder you from being as productive as you would like to be, and can often cause you to become distracted.

Distraction

DISTRACTION *A thing that prevents someone from concentrating on something else*

Let's paint a picture: Candice is sitting at her desk at work, trying to get a few things done. She has two big reports due, so she has both of them open on her desktop, alternating between them and trying to make some headway. In between she has to take care of her day-to-day tasks. She also has her emails open, and reads each pop-up as it comes up to see if there's anything important. She also has a few internet tabs open, for research on her reports, as well as Facebook. The phone on her desk rings every now and then as both co-workers and clients need a quick word. On top of this, her smartphone is lying on her desk, buzzing every now and then as she gets a message or a phone call from friends and family, social media notifications, and personal emails. There's also the noise in the office, co-workers having loud conversations or stopping at her desk to have a chat.

Does this kind of situation sound familiar? Shockingly, it is the kind of multitasking gymnastics our modern, digital world has made perfectly normal. Sometimes it's also a bit of a coping mechanism. When something is unpleasant to do, we like to take little breaks from it, like scanning Facebook or watching a video on YouTube. Unfortunately, this only makes it take that much longer to complete an important task; these little interruptions can be terribly counter-productive.

As already mentioned, our brains do not cope well with this kind of task-hopping. One study found that it takes 23 minutes and 15 seconds to regain your focus after being interrupted while working. This doesn't include planned breaks or interruptions that relate to the same subject matter. Once you have been distracted and you concentrate on your work again, you are not yet functioning at the same level you were before. The longer the distraction, the further away it takes your mind from what it was focusing on to begin with. And this causes you to make more mistakes in your work.

Think about how much you'd get done in an hour working on a document with all of this going on. Now think about an hour working on a document with absolutely nothing else bothering you. Do you think you would get it done faster?

If you spend just one hour a day dealing with distractions, and you eliminated those distractions, you would have an extra hour a day to do something that really matters to you – like leaving work earlier to spend time with your loved ones, or getting some downtime to relax and give your mind a break.

Types of distractions

There are many types of distractions – some of them come from outside (like a phone call) and some of them come from us (like lacking the motivation to get things done).

Most distractions are so part of our everyday lives that we don't even notice them. We might switch off our phones in order to get away from people, but we don't notice that when we do try to concentrate, our minds are on something else, or we procrastinate because we don't want to deal with tough or menial tasks. Everyone's situation is unique: your environment, the people around you, your personality, your phone, your email; whatever is going on in your life at any given time influences how well you are able to focus.

So to get an idea of how much you are getting distracted, and how big your problem is, let's do the following exercise. In these two lists, tick off whichever distractions apply to you. When you are done, see how many things actually affect your concentration – is it more than five, more than 10? The purpose of this exercise is just to get you thinking about what's happening on a daily basis while you are attempting to focus.

In your surroundings	Yes	No
Is your workplace untidy, making it hard to find things or causing you irritation?		
Is your workplace noisy?		
Are you often interrupted by people walking past or coming to have a quick word?		
Does your phone ring often for work-related matters?		
Does your phone ring often for personal matters?		
Do you get a lot of notifications on your phone for things like apps?		
Do you check your phone every time it makes a sound?		
Do you dislike the atmosphere of the area in which you work?		
Is the lighting insufficient, causing you to strain your eyes?		
Is your chair uncomfortable?		
Do you have low energy levels?		
Do you sleep less than eight hours?		
Do you drink a lot of energy drinks and coffee that eventually make it harder for you to sit still or concentrate?		
Do you eat unhealthy foods with empty calories?		

Do you lead a sedentary life with little in the way of exercise?		

In your mind	Yes	No
Are you an emotional person?		
Are you easily upset and stay that way for a while?		
Do you struggle to concentrate when you are upset?		
Do you procrastinate often?		
Do you feel unmotivated?		
Do you find work unappealing?		
Do you have a tendency to daydream?		

If you answered yes to many of these questions, it's obvious that you have a fair amount of distractions that are keeping you from being as productive as you would otherwise be. The good news is that most of these are things you have at least some control over, and now that you know about them, you can start doing something about them!

Figuring out what your biggest distraction is

Do you know what your biggest distraction is? The thing that is eating up the most of your time? The best way to find out is to keep a time log. While this can be a bit time-consuming, you need only keep it up for about a week, and it's definitely worth it. A time log will provide a very detailed and revealing look at exactly how you spend your time – how much you actually work, how much time you spend on things you really shouldn't be spending that much time on, and what the biggest culprits are.

The time log

"Productivity is never an accident. It is always the result of a commitment to excellence, intelligent planning, and focused effort."
– Paul J. Meyer

The following is a short example of a time log. Change the time increments and length to suit you; these are only a guideline. For those who tend to do a lot of multitasking, smaller time increments will work much better, so adjust yours to 15-minute intervals. Likewise, if you have fewer tasks, use bigger increments. The best way to keep it filled in accurately is to print it out and keep it next to you. Try to be detailed so that it can really reveal what's eating away at your time; and make little notes about everything that you do. For example, if you often pause to go onto social media, you need not time it exactly, just write a small note of 'SM'. Be very honest when you fill it in; the answer might be a big eye-opener.

	Mon	Tue	Wed	Thu	Fri	Sat	Sun
07:30-08:00							
08:00-08:30							
08:30-09:00							
09:00-09:30							
09:30-10:00							

When you have completed the time log, it's time to cast an eagle eye over it and identify what's causing you to lose focus. Create a list, and at the top put the main culprits – the things that kept you distracted the longest, and made it harder to regain your focus afterwards.

Then, for each distraction, ask yourself why this distracted you – and write down ways that you could possibly avoid this type of distraction. Also pay attention to how long the distraction persisted.

Lastly, identify the scenarios in which you were able to accomplish the most and ask yourself why. Were you in a more positive mood that day? Had you slept better? Was the environment quieter?

After you have completed this exercise you should have a really good understanding of what's causing you to lose focus in the bigger scheme of things – is social media addiction your problem, is the environment you work in not allowing you to get much done? Once you have recognised and solved some of your biggest problems, you have already gone a long way in channelling your working hours to be more productive, thus freeing up more time for yourself.

12 common distractions and how to get rid of them

Here's a list of some everyday distractions, with some handy advice to avoid them.

1. Fear of being offline

One of the sillier side effects of our digital culture is how addicted we've become to our phones. It's even reached the extent where people go to technology rehab (and have to check in their electronic devices at the door). Stop the madness! If you have to impulsively pick up your phone every time it makes a peep, just switch it off. Don't worry, it'll get easier with time – it may even become a habit when you work.

Unfortunately, you can't switch off your computer when you're working on it, but you can close unnecessary tabs, especially in your browser. If you don't have YouTube open, you won't be tempted to "quickly" watch a video.

2. Noise

If you can't concentrate when there's any sound near you, go somewhere quiet. If you can't, try putting in ear buds and listening to music. If the lyrics distract you, get some music without any. Noise-cancelling headphones are great.

Classical music is also a great way to relax and get your mind into a more creative space.

Did you know?

Some studies have shown that classical music relaxes cows and makes them produce more milk.

3. Stress

There are a number of breathing exercises and mindfulness techniques you could try to calm a busy mind. For instance, sit up straight in your chair with your eyes closed for just a moment. Breathe in deeply and feel the air rush into your lungs, counting four seconds. Hold your breath for 12 seconds and concentrate on how your heart beats. Release your breath for 8 seconds and imagine all toxic stress leaving your body as you do.

If this is a strong problem for you, and you would like a number of additional methods to switch off your busy mind (and ultimately sleep better!), search on Amazon for "Sleep Secrets: Switch off your brain, sleep better and feel refreshed in 9 easy steps".

4. Sitting for too long

You're already pushing your body into doing something it doesn't want to when you make it sit still for eight-plus hours at a time (for those of us with office jobs, anyway).

Our bodies are made to move, not keep still. The unhealthy consequences of all this sitting have become more and more apparent, and the experts have advised us to begin doing some work standing up. Not only does this have health benefits, but it is believed to be more productive in terms of thinking; walking is even recommended to do when studying since it gets more oxygen going through the system and to the brain.

If you're slightly horrified at the idea of spending so much time standing up, at the very least think of ergonomics. You have to get yourself a desk and chair that are comfortable – in other words your back is supported, and you don't begin to suffer from backaches halfway through the day – this is absolutely not conducive to optimal focus. And remember, it's not just about giving a certain amount of time to a task – you want to be at your best so you complete it as well as possible. Also, take breaks and stretch!

5. Lousy atmosphere

If you find it difficult to concentrate due to workspace that lacks inspiration, try working somewhere else – like outside in the fresh air. The move doesn't even have to be permanent; sometimes we just need a brief change of scenery to cure the monotony. You could also spruce up your desk a bit. Get a plant – they're known as instant pick-me-ups: studies have found that ornamental plants and flowers have a soothing effect.

6. Rumbling tummy

Keep some snacks in your drawer in case you start getting hungry before your next meal, and spend the time leading up to it wondering what you're going to eat. Since feeding itself is one of your body's main priorities, hunger tends to override anything else that's going on.

Healthy snacks are always best: things like nuts, fruit or yoghurt.

7. Unmotivated

Motivation to accomplish certain things in life is deeply personal and unique to each individual. If you find yourself lacking a bit in this department, try making a mental list of reasons why you want to get something done, and think about them when you're feeling unmotivated. You could even write down something you find inspirational and stick it up somewhere for you to see.

You can also use positive visualisation. It's what they tell golfers when they're feeling the pressure during a game. Visualise the entire swing and the ball going into the hole. Do this for yourself with what you ultimately want to achieve.

8. Feeling like running away

By this time in your life you would've heard multiple people say that Rome wasn't built in a day. This is because it's true. So when you're facing a really, dauntingly complicated task – break it up into manageable bits, and do it bit by bit (and don't think about the thing in its entirety – it'll just scare you again). Before you know it, you'll be done.

9. Under- and over-stimulation

If a task is boring you, try to keep your mind engaged by making it more enjoyable. Research has shown that when confronted with a task that you strongly dislike, doing something you truly enjoy while you tackle the task can make the experience much more bearable, and possibly even trick your brain into enjoying it. Put on the radio or sit somewhere you find relaxing, like outside. And if it's really stressful, slow down and make yourself a cup of tea.

10. Crazy long to-do lists

If you have 50 different things to do, create a smaller, more immediate list with only the three things you're prioritising. Only look at that list. When you cross something off, put something else on. The shorter list avoids the panic attack you get from having to look at a big list frequently.

11. The big procrastinator

If you notice that you're putting something off, consider the reasons why. Usually it is because it is either too easy or too difficult. It could also be simply because you are too tired, or don't enjoy doing that particular task. Once you have figured out why, rationalise it to yourself. For instance, if it is because it is too daunting or difficult, like writing a report that requires a lot of research, try breaking it up into manageable chunks, and doing it chapter by chapter.

12. Fear of committing

When you're really dreading doing something because you just know it is going to take hours, think about this: you won't notice the time go by when you're focusing. The brain is pretty good about getting on with it once you've got the ball rolling. This means not ruining your flow every five minutes by checking your phone or opening another tab in your browser.

"Once you are able to focus on an activity, you begin to act in that activity with amazing fluidness, as if the activity is running itself and you are just flowing along with it."
– Brian Bruya

Chapter 2
A step-by-step guide to master time management and focus

So now that you're equipped with a few tips to avoid distractions around you, and have a better sense of what focus really is, it's time to put a plan into action to get focused, maximise your productivity and manage your time better. The following steps are meant to do just that, so take some time to execute them one by one. Remember, the goal here is not to work more; it's to use your time better.

Step 1: Realise the importance of time

We all tend to have that mindset of "I'll just deal with it later" when there's something unpleasant that has to be done. The unfortunate side effect of this kind of attitude is that it just adds unnecessary pressure and stress to your life, and more importantly, nothing ever gets done. There will always be more to do; this is an unfortunate fact about the fast pace of our lives.

So take a minute to realise the importance of time in your life. It's something that, once spent, you can never get back. Every new day, you are given a fresh 24 hours to use however you see fit. Use this time to spend on things that are important to you. Think about what you want to incorporate into your life: is it time with your kids, exercise, client relationships, training your staff, getting a degree? Then schedule time every day to dedicate to that goal. When you have incorporated what you value into every day, how can every day not be a success?

Step 2: Set a goal

"A goal without a plan is just a wish."
– Antoine de Saint-Exupery

Needless to say, it's important to have goals in order to avoid just floating through life (unless that's your thing). But goals are also important to keep you motivated. You have to think about why you're doing something. This doesn't necessarily have to mean writing down your life goals right now (unless you already have them all figured out). You can break it up into five-year goals, one-year goals, or even monthly goals. These shouldn't be goals you think you should accomplish, or things other people are pushing you to do, but things that *you* want to do. Thinking about goals that are important to you will be that extra kick in the rear you need to achieve them. So think about the timeframe you want to work in, and write down your goals. You can also stick them up somewhere as reminders to keep you motivated.

Here are some goal examples:

Month-to-month goal:
  • Get more clients to make more money!

Semester goal:
  • *Get at least 75% for each subject!*

One-year goal:
  • *Get 75% average!*

Two-year goal:

- Save enough money to holiday in Tahiti

Three-year goal:
- *Get my degree cum laude!*
-

Step 3: Get organised

"For every minute spent organising, an hour is earned."
– Benjamin Franklin

Now it's time to get organised. This comes more naturally to some folk than others, but it's very easy to do if you can just take the few minutes to do it. You'll feel a lot better afterwards too.

Make a to-do list with every task/activity that you need to get done. Most of us will have one of these already, in some form or another. If you don't have everything written down, don't worry, you can add things as you remember them and as you get new things to do. It's very important to write things down if you want to stay neatly organised. It'll also save you time wasted trying to remember what it was that you had to do.

Your to-do list can take many forms: a diary, your phone, a desk calendar (which is very convenient when you want to jot something down), or just stick a magnetised memo pad to your fridge – whatever gives you the easiest access, so you're not tempted to leave writing things down until later. You might think you'll be able to remember it, but most times people just remember that they were supposed to remember something, not what it actually was.

This is where you'll find one fantastic perk of the digital age: reminders. Set reminders on your computer or phone calendars to keep you aware of approaching deadlines and projects.

However, some people find to-do lists only add unnecessary pressure. An alternative to this form of organisation is to rely solely on a calendar that dictates when you should do what in order to get everything done. You can break down your day into as small as 15-minute increments.

Step 4: Prioritise

"You have exactly the same number of hours per day that were given to Helen Keller, Pasteur, Michaelangelo, Mother Teresa, Leonardo da Vinci, Thomas Jefferson, and Albert Einstein."
– H. Jackson Brown Jr.

It can be a little overwhelming when you have a lot to do, but just take a deep breath and relax – everything doesn't have to be done all at the same time. All you need to do is prioritise the tasks on your to-do list, so you have the all-important starting point. And since you can't do everything at once, that's the only point you need to focus on. Once you have this, you are spared the angst (and probably the related procrastination) of not knowing where to begin.

If it's not immediately apparent to you what takes priority over what, here's a little presidential lifehack to get you on your way. It's called the Eisenhower box.

Very important/time-sensitive	Very important/not time-sensitive
Not important/time-sensitive	Not important/not time-sensitive

Start with the first item on your to-do list. In which one of the categories in the box does it fall?

- **Very important/time-sensitive**

  Absolutely essential to get done by a specific deadline.

  Examples: Reports or projects that have to be submitted by a deadline, agendas that have to be planned for meetings at specified times, proposals that have to be submitted to clients by a deadline.

  Solution: Organise these in order of their deadlines.

- **Very important/not time-sensitive**

Absolutely essential to get done, but doesn't have a specific deadline.

Examples: Getting your website up and running, cold calling to get new clients, refresher courses to keep up with advances in industry.

Solution: Give it a deadline yourself.

- **Not important/time-sensitive**

  Not essential to get done or to achieve your goal, but comes with a deadline.

  Examples: Things pushed on you by colleagues but that don't actually affect you, answering emails, admin tasks.

  Solution: Ask yourself if tasks in this block can be delegated and if they are actually necessary in moving towards your goals.

- **Not important/not time-sensitive**

  Not essential to get done and doesn't have a deadline.

  Examples: Reorganising the filing system, meetings, events.

  Solution: Ask yourself if this can be deleted from your list completely.

Do the same exercise with the rest of the tasks on your to-do list. When you are done, you'll have the important tasks organised by deadline, and eliminated or delegated the inessential.

Step 5: Plan, plan, plan

Once you have determined what the biggest, most important and time-sensitive task is – do it first! Get it out of the way. This is by far what will most likely lead to procrastination. It is also most likely what will be causing you the most stress. Think of it this way – the peace of mind you will get from completing this task timeously and well will make other tasks seem easy in comparison, and you will have the added bonus of not having that little monster at the back of your mind gnawing on your subconscious as you worry unnecessarily about getting that task done. This is a great philosophy to approach your day with, and will automatically give you some direction and save you from being indecisive about where to begin. And the bonus is, as soon as you are finished with it, your day has already been extremely productive!

When you dedicate time to something, do exactly that – dedicate it. This means nothing else gets done in between, and distractions are minimised as much as possible. Reserve checking your emails for an hour in the morning and afternoon, or whatever suits you – don't stop what you're doing to check new messages. Also schedule in breaks and use them to get up and moving, it'll keep your energy levels up.

Get into the habit of taking 10 minutes or 30 minutes each morning to set out your day, so that you can be confident of getting everything done that you need to, and you don't waste time being indecisive about where to begin.

"Many fine things can be done in a day, if you don't always make that day tomorrow." - Unknown

Step 6: Set deadlines

If something doesn't have its own deadline – give it one. Giving yourself an open-ended timeframe will inevitably lead to procrastination, as there is nothing pushing you to get it done. This will also keep your workflow going and subconsciously keep you in check.

Step 7: Stop multitasking!

Your brain functions at its best when it can focus on one thing at a time for an extended period – this means sticking to your plan and not interrupting yourself with anything else. If this hasn't sunk in yet, re-read Chapter 1.

Equally important, this helps you to only think about one thing at a time, which comes in handy when you are trying to avoid the panic of a massive workload. Follow your timetable meticulously, and make sure to allow for tea breaks or short relaxation periods as well.

Step 8: Find your sweet spot

If you're a morning person, and that's when you do your best thinking, schedule the more difficult stuff for then. Same goes for the night owls. Everyone is different, so recognise where you fit in and use it to your advantage.

Step 9: Use your energy wisely

Learn to recognise situations that take up energy unnecessarily – and avoid them. You need to keep your energy for the things that matter. Your time is precious and should be treated as such. If there is a meeting you have been requested to attend but you honestly question whether or not you should be involved, speak to your manager and explain how your time would be better utilised on the project you are currently working on. They will appreciate your forward-thinking and your productivity.

Step 10: Take care of yourself mentally and physically

Even for those of us who absolutely love to work, sometimes your mind and body won't quite agree with you, and if you just keep going, you will eventually reach a low point when you shut down mentally or even physically.

In addition to this, the longer you keep it up, the harder it will be for you to focus, because your brain can get tired too.

"You'll never change your life until you change something you do daily. The secret of your success is found in your daily routine."
– John C. Maxwell

Focus your mind

Take breaks – proper ones! Go on holiday, veg on the couch or string up a hammock outside. Taking care of your brain is important. Burn-out happens when you just keep going; take a minute and just breathe, sending much-needed oxygen to your brain. The ability to calm yourself can come in very handy when you're under pressure.

Focus your body

Your body and mind are connected. When you have a healthy body, your brain's performance will be that much more optimal. That's why it's so crucial to keep a tab on what you put into your body, as well as how you take care of it physically.

Get active!

Your body wants to move – it was built to do so. But our lifestyles are simply not accommodating that fact, since by far the majority of us have jobs where we sit down in the same position all day. The only time we get to move is at home, but which time many of us are simply too tired to exercise. But this is incredibly necessary to keep functioning at your best. The standard recommended exercise is 150 minutes of moderate aerobic activity every week; that's about 30 minutes from Monday to Friday. But even 10 minutes is better than nothing. And gymming isn't the only solution; you can go for a quick jog around the block or even just get out the jumping rope. Or you can incorporate it into your day – take a walk around lunchtime instead of sitting at your desk, take the stairs instead of the elevator, wash your car yourself instead of taking it to the carwash.

Exercise is also good to fight depression and keep us happy, as it causes the release of endorphins – a happy hormone.

Eat right

Your diet has a massive impact on your energy levels and how clearly you are able to think. Plainly put: if you eat crap, you'll feel crap. This doesn't mean eat less, it just means eat right.

It's long been debated about what is the leading cause of increasing disease and expanding waistlines, some blame sugar and some blame fat or meat. The fact is, your mind needs energy to work just as much as your body. That doesn't mean eating an energy bar when you feel tired in the afternoon, it means sticking to the low GI spectrum of the menu. Low GI foods release energy slowly, over a period of time – this means you have sustained energy, and you won't get the "after-lunch slump". By contrast, high GI foods release a big dose of energy quickly, and your body loses that energy just as quickly, leaving you feeling hungrier and tired sooner.

If you're interested in making a real change, it's worth doing some research on the topic to work out a meal plan that'll get your body in optimum condition. It might take some trial and error to find what works for you, but believe me – it'll change your life if you can get it right.

Superfoods – not all food is made equal

SUPERFOOD *A nutrient-rich food considered to be especially beneficial for health and wellbeing*

Some foods are nutritionally dense superfoods that give your body lovely little doses of pure goodness, while other foods don't do all that much. It's definitely worth knowing what the superfoods are, so you're able to incorporate them into your diet as often as possible. Remember, variety is the spice of life – the more different colours of fresh fruit and veggies you eat, the better!

10 foods that will nourish your mind

Here's some food for thought, literally:

- ◆ *Wholegrains* Provide a steady supply of energy, making your brain more alert.

- ◆ *Blackcurrants* Lots of vitamin C, which is thought to be an excellent mental booster.

- ◆ *Blueberries* These little balls of antioxidant goodness have a host of benefits for your body and then some. Some studies even indicate that they might improve memory.

- ◆ *Oily fish* like salmon and tuna – excellent for your brain!

- ◆ *Pumpkin seeds* Good for thinking.

- ◆ *Broccoli* Good for cognitive function.

- ◆ *Dark green leafy veggies* Lots of vitamin E, which protects cell membranes, keeping the whole cell healthy.

- ◆ *Berries* Thought to help slow down cognitive decline.

- ◆ *Nuts* Another great source of vitamin E.

- ◆ *Avocado* Lost of monounsaturated fat (the healthy kind), which contributes to healthy blood flow (including to your brain). They also help lower blood pressure.

4 ways to a healthier you

If making a drastic change isn't your thing though, here are a few handy tips that you can incorporate into your lifestyle to give you that extra edge.

- ◆ *Cut the sugar* Save those fizzy drinks for special occasions. They contain as much as nine teaspoons of sugar (that's the recommended daily limit for an adult male). Followers of sugar-free diets will tell you it makes your thinking foggier.

- ◆ *Hydrate* How much water you should drink every day depends on a few things, like your weight and activity level, but it's generally conceded to be between 1.5 and 2 litres. Your body is about 60% water, and it's necessary in many of your bodily functions, so staying hydrated keeps you at 100%.

- ◆ *Give the fried food a skip* There's nothing nutritional about it, and it's really terrible for your health. Really. Eating fresh is always best.

- ◆ *Sleep!* Your brain needs this time to recharge – let it.

Step 11: Get rid of the clutter

Part of becoming more efficient at important tasks is getting rid of unimportant ones. This includes everything from spending too much time on checking emails to accepting too many tasks delegated to you by others. For some people, it's really hard to say no, but try to remember that you're saying no to the task, not the person. Know when you can't take on anything more.

Additionally a cluttered desk or environment can immediately make you feel as though there is too much to do. Take one day a month to throw out all the stuff you really don't need. Even better, give it away! Your environment will be more zen-like and you will feel great for helping someone out!

Step 12: Stop to smell the roses

While it's great to be productive and tick off tasks on a to-do list, don't forget to try and enjoy what you're doing once in a while.

We're hardwired to feel satisfied when something's been completed successfully, but we also get a lot of motivation from progress in our tasks – savour these small milestones, they've been shown to increase motivation and productivity in the long run.

At the end of every day on your way home from work, turn off the car radio and think for a few moments about 3 things you accomplished today. This can be the smallest accomplishment such as *'taking the time in the morning to properly organise your day'*, *'making that phone call you were really just putting off'*, or *'creating an email filing system'*

"The key to realizing a dream is to focus not on success but significance – and then even the small steps and little victories along your path will take on greater meaning." - Oprah Winfrey.

Chapter 3
Get your own system going to maximise your productivity

Now that you have a better understanding of how focus works, how it applies to you as an individual, and have taken the steps to become more focused, you can start tailoring a system that works perfectly for you. The downloadable action plan will help you on your way to tailoring your own time management masterpiece.

Recognise what distracts you and prevent those distractions from occurring, and implement the steps necessary to effectively manage your time and focus. Every step may not work for you, so try them all and keep what works.

The more you do this, the better you will become at it. It will become habitual. It's true what they say: practice makes perfect.

Conclusion

Thank you again for downloading this book!

I sincerely hope this book has a positive impact on your life. While it is a guide to become more productive and focused, the ideal end result is to help you manage your life more efficiently, so that you have more time to do the things that really matter to you and can lead a more balanced life.

Finally, if you enjoyed his book, please take the time to share your thoughts and post a review on Amazon. It'd be greatly appreciated.

Thank you and good luck!

Dene Chittenden

http://www.mellowzoo.com

Preview Of 'Sleep Secrets Switch off your brain, sleep better, and feel refreshed in just 9 easy steps'

And so it begins

It's 2am on a Monday morning. You're still awake. Wide awake. Staring at the ceiling yet again, worrying every 10 minutes about how much time you have left to sleep before you have to get up for work. The more you try to close your eyes and concentrate on falling asleep, the harder it seems to be. It's a vicious cycle. You're exhausted and frustrated, but your brain just won't 'click' off.

I've been there: for six months I relied on the little sleep I got to keep functioning. If I managed four hours, it was a great night, but when it started dropping to two hours, then one hour, then 20 minutes, I knew I had to do something! Anything! I was in a state of turmoil, and it seemed as though nothing was helping, which simply made my frustration worse. It started affecting my mood, my work and my relationships. I had to find a way. It took months trying to figure out what it was that was keeping me awake. I was willing to try anything out of sheer desperation.

Then one day I got it right.

Is this the book for you?

If, like me, you are at that point where you are feeling frustrated and you just need to sleep, then this book is for you. I have taken the time to meticulously compile everything I've tried into one small, easy-to-follow guide in the hopes that my experiences could somehow help you. I've also included short action plans for each step to really give you a head start. You will learn how to give yourself every advantage to fall asleep, from getting your environment ready to monitoring your patterns with a sleep log and trying various techniques on how to relax a busy mind.

The purpose of this book is purely to help you figure out what is keeping you awake and how we can possibly fix that together.

So if you're ready for some serious shut-eye, then let's get started!

Search the Amazon Kindle store for "Sleep Secrets: Switch off your brain, sleep better and feel refreshed in 9 easy steps".